For a better life
The Mind

A Book on Self-Empowerment

Compiled by
M. M. Walia

NEW DAWN PRESS, INC.
USA• UK• INDIA

NEW DAWN PRESS GROUP

Published by New Dawn Press Group
New Dawn Press, Inc., 244 South Randall Rd # 90, Elgin, IL 60123
e-mail: sales@newdawnpress.com

New Dawn Press, 2 Tintern Close, Slough, Berkshire, SL1-2TB, UK
e-mail: salesuk@newdawnpress.org

New Dawn Press (An Imprint of Sterling Publishers (P) Ltd)
A-59, Okhla Industrial Area, Phase-II, New Delhi-110020, India
e-mail: info@sterlingpublishers.com
www.sterlingpublishers.com

For a better life – The Mind

© 2006, Sterling Publishers (P) Ltd
ISBN 1 84557 580 6

All rights are reserved. No part of this publication may be
reproduced, stored in a retrieval system or transmitted, in any
form or by any means, mechanical, photocopying, recording or
otherwise, without prior written permission of the publisher.

PRINTED IN INDIA

A Controlled Mind

A well trained and controlled mind
stands a man in good stead
better than armies.
It saves him from cowardice
as well as perils.
Even though you have not conquered
in battles, the world,
you become the world-conquerer
when you have conquered your mind.
– Swami Chinmayananda

The Holy Triad

- The holy triad—the body, mind and soul that man comprises, is a wonderous synergy of these three elements. How the body and mind mutually influence each other is well known. To understand that the soul has an overpowering relevance in the lives of human beings, needs spiritual enlightenment.

- Besides other important functions, the mind generates thoughts. "As the man thinks, so he becomes" is an established truth.

- ❖ The uncontrolled mind leads to the dissipation of the tremendous energy that human beings have. Man who has control over his mind acquires powers wherein even the sky is not the limit.

What is Mind?

- The mind is popularly defined as that which thinks, knows, feels and wills. For our purpose, the Mind can be defined as that which is conscious of an object, and consciousness can be defined as the relation between subject and object.

- Consciousness is subjective, but it can only arise when attention is present. Along with every consciousness arises certain mental constituents, otherwise called mental factors. Love,

Hate, Greed, Anger, and Worry, are some of them.

- ❖ Only one consciousness can arise at a time, namely, only one Mind can arise at a time. One consciousness disappears before the next consciousness arises.

- ❖ When there are so many competing outside objects, the stimulus that claims attention at the moment will produce the corresponding Mind. The Mind works very fast. It is said that it takes about a billionth of a second for the Mind to arise, and it immediately disappears.

- ❖ The human personality or ego consists of Body and Mind.
- ❖ It is the Mind that wants and says to drink, and it is the Body that drinks. It is the Mind that wants to eat, and it is the Body that eats. In every matter, it is the Mind that directs and the Body that obeys. All verbal and physical actions are motivated by the subjective Mind.
- ❖ Mind is the finer body within this gross body. The physical body is, as it were, only the outer crust of the mind. The Mind is the finer part of the body, and one affects the other. It

is for this reason that physical illness often affects the mind and mental illness or tension often affects the body.

❖ Behind the mind is the *Atman*, the real Self of man.

— **Meditation and Concentration**

Ven P. Preech Thaharn

The Senses

"The turbulent senses, O Arjuna, do violently snatch away the mind of even a wise man, striving after perfection.

    For the mind which follows in the wake of the wandering senses, carries away his discrimination, as the wind carries off its course, a boat on the waters."

— *Bhagavad Gita*

Gems of Wisdom
by Sri Sathya Sai Baba

❖ Why, then, is there this call for control of the mind (*Manonigraham*)? *Nigraham* (Control) really means being indifferent to the vagaries of the mind. It is difficult to control the mind, even as it is difficult to confine air in one's grasp. Likewise, how can anyone control the mind which is all-embracing in the vastness of its range and comprehension? When it is realised that the mind is made up of thoughts and doubts, the elimination of thoughts is the means of restraining the mind. Thoughts are associated with desires. As long as desires remain, one cannot have *vairaagva* (detachment). It is necessary to limit desires.

❖ The human mind is exceedingly small, but it can comprehend this vast universe. The mind appears as an insignificant speck in the universe, but the universe is immanent in this minuscule mind. It would appear as if the universe and the mind were telling each other: "I am that" and "that is me".

❖ It is not correct to consider the combination of the body, intellect, mind and senses as a human being. Mind is something we possess, the body is our vesture, and intelligence and senses are dealt with by us. All of them are ours. We have the capability of manipulating them. The mind, on its own, moves on the right path, but the senses and the outer world drag it astray.

❖ The mind is the mischief-maker; it jumps from doubt to doubt; it creates obstacles in the path of spirituality. It weaves a net and gets entangled in it.

It is ever discontented; it chases after a hundred things and runs away from another hundred. So take up the task of training it into an obedient servant.

❖ The mind is like a sheet of paper; once rolled in one direction, it will always roll along in that direction only. You will have to roll it in the opposite direction in order to flatten it.

❖ The mind assumes the form of the objects with which it is attached. If it gets fixed on small things, it becomes small; when fixed on grand things, then it becomes grand.

❖ There are nine lamps that can free the mind from darkness: Listening, Adulation, Remembrance, Showing Respect, Ceremonial Worship, Paying Obeisance, Service, Friendliness, Self-Surrender.

❖ The mind will be a means of liberation when it is rid of the impurities residing in it. All spiritual exercises are designed only to clean the mind.

- ❖ It is indeed a tragedy that the mind of a man makes him sacrifice the good things in life, like the love of God, fear of sin and social morality.
- ❖ Never allow your mind to judge things and men. To say: This is good, that is bad, this is right, that is wrong ... is depreciatory judgement.

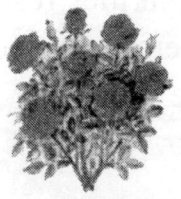

The Mind Creates

"Philosophy tells us that the mind decides, not merely the goodness or badness of a thing or experience, it creates all things and all experiences. Without the mind, there can be no object or feeling or emotion. No mind, no matter! The mind revels in name and form; it imposes name and form, and thus helps in creating things and experiences. It cannot contact or operate upon anything without name and form. That is why the mind is helpless when meditation has to be done on the nameless and the formless. It clings to name-form, ever. Mental pictures have concretised themselves as objects and as ideas; so, the *Shruthis* declare, "*Yad bhavam, tad bhavathi*" — as the mind operates, so, the matter is decided."

— *Sathya Sai Baba*

Mind – Its Faculty and Its Limitation

The mind in its essence is a consciousness which measures, limits, cuts out forms of things from the indivisible whole and contains them as if each were a separate integer. Even with what exits only as obvious parts and fractions, the Mind establishes this function of its ordinary commerce that they are things with which it can deal separately and not merely as aspects of a whole. For, even when it knows that they are not things in themselves, it is obliged to deal with them as if they were things in themselves; otherwise it could not subject them to its own characteristic activity. It is this essential characteristic of the Mind which conditions the workings of all its operative powers, be it conception, perception, sensation or the dealings of creative thought. It conceives, perceives, senses things as if rigidly cut out from a background or a mass, and employs them as fixed units of the material given to it for creation or possession. All its action and enjoyment deal thus with wholes that form part of a greater whole, and these subordinate wholes again are broken up into parts which are also treated as wholes for the particular purposes they serve. The mind may divide, multiply, add, subtract, but it cannot get beyond the limits of this mathematics. If it goes beyond and tries to conceive a real whole, it loses itself in a foreign element; it falls from its own firm ground into the ocean of the intangible, into the abyss of the infinite where it can neither perceive, conceive, sense nor deal with its subject for creation and enjoyment. For if the Mind appears sometimes to conceive, to perceive, to sense or to enjoy with possession the infinite, it is only in seeming and always in a figure of the infinite. What it does vaguely possess is to imply a formless *Vast* and not the real spaceless infinite. The Mind cannot possess the infinite, it can only suffer it or be possessed by it. The possession of the infinite cannot come except by an ascent to those super mental planes, nor the knowledge of it, except by an inert submission of the Mind to the descending messages of the Truth-Conscious Reality.

This essential faculty and the essential limitation that accompanies it are the truths of the Mind.

— *Sri Aurobindo*

Food for the Mind

The foods which augment vitality, energy, strength, health, cheerfulness and appetite, which are savoury and oleaginous, substantial and agreeable, are liked by the 'sattvika'.

The foods that are bitter, sour, saline, excessively hot, pungent, dry and burning are liked by the 'rajasika' and are productive of pain, grief and disease.

That which is stale and tasteless, stinking, cooked overnight, refuse and impure is the food liked by the *'tamasika'*.

— *Bhagavad Gita*

The Power of the Mind

- Though the mind is not a free agent, its powers are simply incalculable. If man has smashed the invisible atom and released its power, if man has realised the unseen 'Higher Self' and become illumined, it is through the powers of the mind that he has done these things; and so with all his other achievements in the diverse fields which fall between these two poles of attainment. In fact, the mind is omnipresent. Each mind is a part of the universal mind. Each mind is connected with every other mind. Therefore each mind, wherever it may be, can be in communication with the whole world.

- ◆ The mind has the power of looking back into itself. With the help of the mind we can analyse the mind, and see what is going on in the mind.

Constituents of the Mind

❖ The mind is the compound of three substantive forces called *gunas*, viz, '*sattva*', '*rajas*' and '*tamas*'. These *gunas* are also the basic constituents of the entire universe, physical and mental. *Sattva* is the principle of poise conducive to purity, knowledge and joy. *Rajas* is the principle of motivity, leading to activity, desire, and restlessness. *Tamas* is the principle of inertia, resulting in inaction, dullness and delusion. *Tamas* causes the mind to move on a low level; *Rajas* scatters the mind and makes it restless and *Sattva* gives it a higher direction.

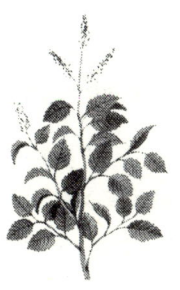

Operating Planes

❖ 'Conscious' and 'subconscious' indicate different planes on which the mind operates. On the conscious plane all work is normally accompanied by the feeling of egoism. On the subconscious plane the feeling of egoism is absent.

❖ There is a still higher plane on which the mind can work. It can go beyond relative consciousness. Just as the subconscious is beneath consciousness, so there is another plane which is above relative consciousness. This is called the 'superconscious' plane. Here also the feeling of egoism is absent, but there is a vast difference between this and the subconscious plane. When the mind passes beyond the plane of relative consciousness, it enters into 'samadhi' or superconsciousness.

❖ The superconscious plane of the mind is the mind in its pure state. In a sense it is then identical with *Atman*. This is why Sri Ramakrishna says: "That which is pure mind is also pure '*buddhi*'; that again is pure *Atman*."

- ❖ These three planes of conscious, subconscious and superconscious, all belong to the same mind. There are not three minds in one person but three levels on which it operates.

- ❖ The question of controlling the mind relates only to the conscious plane, where the mind is normally accompanied by feelings of egoism. We cannot directly control the subconscious mind unless we are established in Yoga. The question of controlling the mind on the superconscious plane does not arise. But the superconscious plane can be reached only by those who have controlled their minds on the conscious and subconscious planes.

Faculties of the Mind

❖ The mind in its functional aspect has four faculties, viz, *'manas'*, *'buddhi'*. *'ahamkara'* and *'chitta'*.

Manas — the cogitating or thinking faculty, which is usually almost entirely wasted, because uncontrolled; however, properly governed, it is a wonderful power. Manas is that modification of the internal instrument (*antahkarana*) which considers the pros and cons of a subject.

Buddhi — the will (sometimes called the intellect). *Buddhi* is that modification of the internal instrument which determines.

Ahamkara — the self-conscious egoism (from Aham). *Ahamkara* is that modification of the inner instrument which is characterised by self-consciousness.

Chitta — the substance in and through which all the faculties act, the floor of the mind as it were; or the sea in which the various faculties are like waves. *Chitta* is that modification of the inner instrument which remembers.

Yoga is the science by which we stop *chitta* from assuming, or becoming transformed into several faculties. As the reflection of the moon on the sea is broken or blurred by the waves, so is the reflection of the *Atman*, the true Self, broken by the mental waves. Only when the sea is stilled to mirror like calmness, can the reflection of the moon be seen, and only when the 'mind-stuff', the *chitta* is controlled to absolute calmness, is the Self to be recognised.

One Pointedness of the Mind

❖ The ordinary conditions of the mind are 'darkened' and 'scattered'. In the darkened state a man feels dull and passive. In the scattered state he feels restless. Through practising the disciplines of yoga the same mind can be 'gathered' and made 'one-pointed'. The whole purpose of mind-control is to make the mind one-pointed. When such a mind is applied to any sphere of activity, in that it shines. Through the practice and development of one-pointedness, the mind reaches the fifth or highest condition called 'concentrated'. In this condition superconsciousness is attained.

— ***The Mind and its Control***
Swami Budhananda

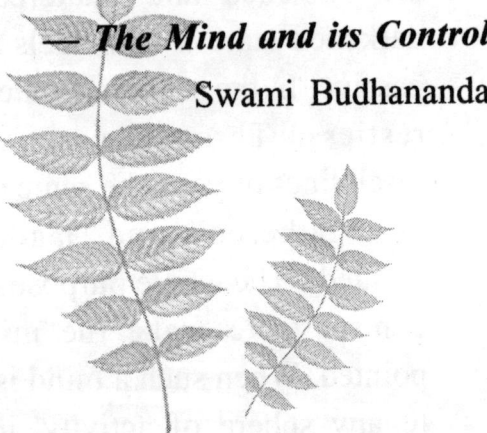

The Mind can make a
hell of heaven or a heaven of hell.
The suffering of each depends,
not upon the factual happenings,
but upon the texture
of each one's mind.
a peaceful mind is a significant
condition of happiness.
An unagitated mind
is itself proof against all sorrows.
Sorrow is nothing but
an agitated condition of the mind.
– Swami Chinmayananda

Mind Control
Difficult but Possible

- All Indian thinking and practice on mind-control are largely based on the following teaching of Sri Krishna:

   Undoubtedly, O Arjuna, the mind is restless and hard to control. But by practice (abhyasa) and dispassion (vairagya) it can be controlled.

- From this teaching, the following three basic facts about mind-control emerge:

- That it has always been an extremely difficult task even for heroic persons of the stature of Arjuna.
- That yet it is possible to control the mind.
- That there are well-defined methods for controlling the mind.

Benefits of Mind Control

- Non-control of mind effectively obstructs integration of personality. A person with an uncontrolled mind will always have a tendency to abnormal developments or to mental disintegration through internal conflict. Even under the most favourable circumstances he will not realise his potential or fulfil expectations.

- On the positive side, at its highest, through control of mind, one can attain spiritual illumination. Short of that, there are many other blessings of life attainable through the control of mind. A controlled mind can easily concentrate. Through concentration of mind one gains knowledge. And knowledge is power.

- One of the spontaneous results of the control of mind is the integration of personality. Such a person succeeds, even in adverse circumstances. A controlled state of mind leads to calmness, and calmness leads to peace of mind. Peace of mind leads to happiness. A happy person makes others happy. The quality of his work improves steadily and he often attains enduring prosperity. It is not that such a person has not to face the trials and tribulations of life. But he never lacks the courage and strength to face them. Society looks up to such a person as an exemplar of good life.

- A person, of controlled mind will be free from mental maladies and physical troubles caused by mental tension.

Absent-Mindedness

Absent-mindedness can be cured only by being mindful of everything, moment to moment. You must "live in the present." You must be aware of the happenings, you must be conscious of the happenings, at every moment. In due course of time, you will be conscious of each happening from the time of your awakening in the morning till the moment you fall asleep.

– *Meditation and Concentration*
Ven P. Preecha Thaharn

How Restless is the Mind?

How hard it is to control the mind! How well has it been compared to the maddened monkey. There was a monkey, restless by his own nature, as all monkeys are. As if that were not enough, someone made him drink freely of wine, so that he became still more restless Then a scorpion stung him. So the poor monkey found his condition worse than ever. To complete his misery, a demon entered into him. The human mind is like that monkey, incessantly active by its own nature; then it becomes drunk with the wine of desire, thus increasing its turbulence. After desire takes possession, comes the sting of the scorpion out of jealousy at the success of others, and last of all, the demon of pride enters the mind, making it think itself of all importance. How hard it is to control such a mind!

—*Swami Vivekananda*

Mind-control Made Easy

To succeed in controlling the mind one must have, in addition to a strong will, faith in oneself. Sri Krishna says in the *Gita* that one must oneself subdue one's weakness and raise oneself by oneself. This teaching must be practised by one who intends to control his mind.

The mind will have to be controlled by the mind itself. The difficulties which we experience in controlling the mind are created by our own mind. The Mind cannot be controlled by artificial means for any length of time. Deliberate, patient, intelligent, systematic hard work according to tested and suitable disciplines is needed.

A Clear Grasp of the Task on Hand

It must be clearly understood and fully accepted that there is no gimmick by which the mind can be controlled. Those who are in a hurry and looking for clever devices may be warned that the mind, a delicate instrument, should be handled very carefully. The entire work of controlling the mind will have to be done by ourselves. No one else can do it for us. We cannot get it done by someone else for a fee. It is our personal task. We must do it ourselves. And we shall need great patience to do it.

Swami Vivekananda teaches: The mind has to be gradually and systematically brought under control. The will has to be strengthened by a slow, continuous, and persevering drill. This is no child's play, no fad to be tried one day and discarded the next. It is a lifetime's work; and the end to be attained is well worth all that it can cost us to reach it; being nothing less than the realization of our absolute oneness with the Divine.

Surely, with this end in view, and with the knowledge that we can certainly succeed, no price can be too great to pay.

A Favourable Inner Climate Needs to be Created

To be able to practise the disciplines leading to the control of the mind, we need to create a favourable inner climate by consciously accepting certain inevitable facts of life. Though inevitable, often enough we do not accept them as such, with the result that unnecessary mental problems are created. But those who want to control their minds must scrupulously avoid loading it with

So they develop unnecessary problems, since there is quite enough of necessary and unavoidable ones.

The impurities of the mind are the strong impulse and emotions like envy, hatred, anger, fear, jealousy, lust, greed, conceit, temptation, etc. born of the two lower *gunas* — *rajas* and *tamas*. These impurities cause disturbances in the mind by creating attachment and aversion, and thus rob it of tranquility.

. . . .

He loves God, not because he desires anything from him, but because He is dear to him, because He is his beloved whom he loves for the sake of love. So long as we expect something, we do not love truly, and the Ideal remains far from us. Only when we have begun to love for the sake of love are. we truely devoted

Have love for your Ideal, whatever you may call Him. Serve Him Faithfully.

Purity of Mind

The player must let his senses come under control. Purity of the mind must be insisted upon if you want control over your mind. The man who is perfectly moral has nothing more to do; he is free. When the food is pure, the mind becomes pure. When the mind becomes pure, memory becomes firm. And when a man is in possession of a firm memory, all the bonds which tie him down to the world are loosened.

Swami Vivekananda

One must go into solitude to attain this Divine love. To get butter from milk you must let it settle in a secluded spot. If it is disturbed too much, the milk will not turn into curd. Next, you must put aside all other duties, sit in a quiet spot, and churn the curd. Only then, do you get butter. Similarly, by meditating on God in solitude, the mind acquires knowledge, dispassion and devotion. Pure knowledge and pure love are one and the same thing. Both lead the

Training the Mind to Behave

The easiest way to get hold of the mind is to sit quiet and let it drift where it will for a while. Then see it, think as if it were a thing entirely apart from yourself. Identify yourself with God, never with matter or with the mind. Picture the mind as a calm lake stretched before you and the thoughts that come and go as bubbles rising and breaking on its surface. Make no effort to control the thoughts, but watch them and follow them in imagination as they float away. This will gradually lessen the circles. For the mind ranges over wide circles of thought and those circles widen out into ever-increasing circles, as in a pond into which a stone is thrown. We want to reverse the process, and starting with a huge circle make it narrower, until at last we can fix the mind on one point and make it stay there. When the identification of yourself with thought and feeling grows less, you can entirely separate yourself from the mind and actually know it to be apart from yourself.

Keeping the Mind Occupied is healthy

...through mere intellect; nor even by the practice of yoga or different kinds of hardships, saying "An idle mind is the... He is to be attained by true and pure, unselfish and single-minded love. God is free. He is not bound by any law. Shri He says "I remain bound to My devotees". A great Saviour declared, "Sacred is love and its lover is God." One can realise and feel this only with a sincere and pure heart. As long as we have selfish desires we cannot expect to have this. It is holy and Divine

Steadfast cultivation of awareness of the highest objective of life, which is the Supreme Spirit, is a potent method of

❖ stewing the mind. In fact when we practise this discipline we shall derive greater benefit from other practices

When this kind of love awakens, one becomes free of worldly ties. But we must not give up hope just because it is hard. However hard it may be from the standpoint of the world, still it must be realised. Without it the heart is but a barren ground. This is our life and this is the only reality in this world. And it is not at all hard for a sincere and true devotee, because his heart is made of love and naturally flows towards the Lord.

Use of the Imagination

Man is endowed with the faculty of imagination. A great deal of our mental troubles and difficulties in controlling the mind arises from our habitual wrong use of this faculty. It is common practice with many of us to indulge in what is called emotional kite-flying, day-dreaming, and wild, meaningless and purposeless speculation of various sorts. Our expectations may be imaginary, without any basis in fact, but they bring us real disappointments. Our fears may be baseless, but they cause genuine trepidation in our heart. Through exercising our power of imagination we make unreal things real for ourselves. And we become victims of worries and concerns for which there is no factual basis. When this habit becomes a hardened one, it is extremely difficult to control the mind. Sometimes, we may not even be aware of the fact that for a good part of our day we live in dreamland, in a world of shadows, and not in that of truth and facts.

Similarly, we require one kind of imagination to counteract another. We require the right imagination to throw out wrong ones.

Swami Chinmayananda on Love

Imagination properly employed
is our greatest friend;
it goes beyond reason
and is the only light that takes

When our hearts are full of love,
The purest of imaginations is the
life is a smiling valley
thought of God
of beauty and joy,
The more we cling to the thought of God,
romantic and divine.
the less will be our trouble

with the mind.

— Swami Vivekananda

Emergency Control Devices

❖ When love rises to swirl around us, and when we re-view in this clear light of love, the very faults get transformed into the essential beauty in them. This is the magic touch of love, the miracle played by love.

love is not love
if it does not serve and sacrifice.

❖ ❖ ❖

understand what a close watch we have to keep on our thoughts and emotions.

❖ Nothing is more exhausting than wrestling with the mind. The more we are exhausted the more turbulent the mind becomes; and ultimately we are swept away. In such a situation a frontal attack on the mind is not very helpful. What should we do then? We should cease to identify ourselves with the mind. If we do this, a tremendous amount of work would have been done.

❖ As long as we identify ourselves with the mind, we cannot control it. The moment we succeed, through philosophic thought, in separating ourselves from the mind, then it has nothing to stand on from where it can make trouble.

Directed Thought

❖ Teaching what we should do when we are being greatly tempted, a Western mystic suggests the following practical measures which can be practised by anyone in distress anywhere in the world. These precepts, with such adaptations as are necessary, will be found helpful in all inner emergencies.

- Follow the example of children when they see a wolf or a bear in the country. They immediately run to the arms of their father or mother, or at least they call out to them for help and assistance. Turn, in similar manner, to God and implore His mercy and His help. This is the remedy that our Lord has taught:

❖ 'Pray that ye enter not into temptation.'

- Psychologically speaking, what we need to ceaselessly call on God, every

---

Every act of love brings happiness; there is no act of love which does not bring peace and blessedness as its reaction. Real existence, real knowledge, real love are eternally connected with one another, the three in one; where one of them is, the others also must be; they are the three aspects of the One without second — the Existence—Knowledge—Bliss."

❖ 'Love is the law of life. He who loves, lives; he who is selfish, is dying. Therefore, love for love's sake.

- breath, being a call and giving birth to another self, there is then no loophole through which the inimical thought can assert itself and be translated into action. The strategy is to cause a more powerful expulsion of involuntary inimical thought. By constant, even frantic, calling to God or to one's own higher self, by repetition of a *mantra*, [if one is initiated], or of a divine name, a higher impulsion is to be set into motion within, is to take care of the emergency.
- Let us first tear ourselves away from the locale of the situation, go out for

---

breath being a call and giving birth to another self, there is then no loophole
love your fellow beings as yourselves. But no reason was forthcoming, no one knows why it would be good to love other beings as ourselves. And you understand why there is an impersonal God, when you learn that the whole world is one — a higher impulsion... I am loving myself. Hence, we understand why we ought not to hurt others.

a brisk long walk in the company of one's higher self, as it were, and try to put our mind onto something elevating and commendable. If for want of faith one cannot cry to God and lay one's inside bare for divine inspection, let us turn to Nature—a flowing river, the sky, the wind, the towering cliff of a mountain, to the vast ocean or the rising sun—and narrate our story candidly and ask for an understanding and power for self-transcendence.

- Better than this, however, will be to communicate one's inner situation to a wise, trustworthy selfless man of character and seek his advice and help. Such a person should be very carefully selected. If a trustworthy person is not available, it is better to fight one's inner battle oneself.

—The Mind and its Control

Swami Budhananda

Yoga

Charity, the performance of one's duty, the observance of vows, general and particular, listening to the scriptures, meritorious acts, and all such works—all these culminate in the control of the mind. The control of the mind is the highest yoga.

— *Bhagavad Gita*

Control of Thoughts

❖ Thought-control in the initial stage does not mean that there will be no thought in the mind at all. A thoughtless state may be a stupid state. In the initial stage, thought-control means developing the capacity deliberately to think good thoughts and to desist from thinking bad or wrong ones.

We are what our thoughts make us; so take care of what you think. Words are secondary. Thoughts live, they travel far. Each thought we think is tinged with our character, so that for the pure and holy man, even his jest or abuse will have the twist of his own love and purity and do good.

❖ In its highest stage, thought-control means complete cessation of thought. As long as we identify ourselves with the ego or the body we cannot reach this stage. What Swami Vivekananda teaches in the following lesson on *pranayama* indicates the processes by which cessation of thought is attained: *"Identify yourself only with God. After a while thoughts will announce their coming, and we shall learn the way they begin and be aware of what we are going to think, just as on this plane we can look out and see a person coming."*

❖ Why should there be repetition? We have not forgotten the theory of *samskaras*, that the sum total of impressions lives in the mind. They become more and more latent but remain there, and as soon as they get the right stimulus, they come out. Molecular vibration never ceases. If and when this universe is destroyed, all the massive vibrations will disappear; the sun, the moon, the stars, and the earth, will melt down; but the vibrations will remain in the atoms. Each atom performs the same function as the big world does. Thus we can understand what is meant by repetition. It is the greatest stimulus that can be given to the spiritual *samskaras*; 'One moment's company in the holy, makes a ship cross this ocean of life.' Such is the power of association. So this repetition of *Om* and thinking of its meaning is like keeping good company in your own mind. Study, and then meditate on what you have studied. Thus light will come to you, the Self will become manifest.

❖ But one must think of *Om*, and of its meaning too. Avoid evil company, because the scars of old wounds are in you, and evil company is just the thing that is necessary to call them out. In the same way we are told that good company will call out the good impressions that are in us, but which have become latent. There is nothing holier in the world than to keep good company, because good impressions tend to come to the surface.

❖ The first manifestation of the repetition and thinking of *Om* is that the introspective power will manifest itself more and more, and all the mental and physical obstacles will begin to vanish.

Control of the Subconscious Mind

❖ We now turn to the control of the subconscious mind, as a natural extension of our work on the conscious level. We have all experienced this strange phenomenon in our life : We know what is right but we cannot act according to it; we know what is wrong but we cannot desist from doing it. We make very good resolutions, but before we are aware of it, like the sand-dyke before a tidal wave, they are washed away. We stand bewildered and frustrated.

❖ So to control the mind, important work needs to be done in the subconscious. On the other hand, if we do not aim at the attainment of life's goal, which is the experience of the superconscious state, we cannot really control our mind, conscious and subconscious. It is only the experience of the superconscious state, or the vision of God, that destroys all the attachments, aversions and delusions, which cause the disturbances and disquiet of the mind.

❖ This is the first part of the study, the control of the unconscious. The next is to go beyond the conscious. Just as unconscious work is beneath consciousness, so there is another work which is above consciousness. When this superconscious state is reached man becomes free and divine, death becomes immortality, weakness becomes infinite power, and iron bondage becomes liberty. That is the goal, the infinite realm, of the superconscious.

The Simplest and the Surest Method of Controlling the Mind

- ❖ So the best way to control the mind is to love God. But if you do not believe in God, then believe in yourself. Exercise your will and transcend the *gunas* by self-effort. By this means also you will gain control of your mind.

❖ In any case, for the believer as for the non-believer, a way of controlling the mind always remains open. There is no greater blessing in life than a controlled state of mind. Let us do our very best to acquire it, for this will lead us to the greatest of blessings.

—**The Mind and its Control**

Swami Budhananda

As the thought, so the mind;

And as the mind, so the man.

A quiet mind produces

a more brilliant intellect.

The quieter the mind,

the sharper the intellect.

— *Swami Chinmayananda*

Mind Development

❖ There are two kinds of mind development and they are called:

- Concentration or *Samatha Bhavana*. *Samatha* means calm; it leads to calm and tranquillity and serenity. No previous knowledge of any doctrine is necessary. You concentrate your mind and you get psychic powers.

- Meditation or *Vipassana Bhavana*. *Vipassana* leads to insight, wisdom, and eventually to Nirvana, which is peace.
- The power and capacities of the human mind are really wonderful and have been the subject of much wonder and speculation through the ages. The source of these powers and capacities is in humans themselves and they can be attained by mental training.
- The Samatha Method of Mental Training is based on concentration. It

requires just average intelligence. There is no need for a college education or even a high-school education. Concentration is a wonderful technique for inducing calm that will help you face the tensions and pressures of everyday life. Concentration may be called relaxation, and per se will produce calmness of mind and body.

❖ The main idea is to shut out external thoughts. After a while, concentration becomes very pleasurable. In due course it will be your ruling passion, your heart's delight, and you will be at it every spare moment; but do not let it interfere with your daily chores.

❖ There are many intensities of concentration ranging from the preliminary or lowest stage to the highest or perfect stage, which is attained after much practice. It is not difficult to achieve the preliminary stage of concentration. When you are reading a book and forget about the external world, you are exhibiting concentration of mind. When you go to the movie and you suddenly lose awareness of the signs which say 'Exit' on the right or left of the screen, you are exhibiting concentration of mind.

Practice of Pranayama

- ❖ We shall notice that when our mind is in a disturbed state, our breathing becomes faster and irregular. One of the ways of quieting the mind is to regularise the breathing. Regular practice of deep breathing helps to develop a stable state of mind.

- ❖ It may be mentioned here that the practice of *pranayama* (restraining the breath in order to get control of the *prana* or vital force) is very helpful for controlling the mind.

Pranayama should, however, be learnt directly from a teacher, and should be practised in a clean atmosphere. Besides, those who do not practice continence, or have a diseased heart, lungs or nervous system, are advised not to practise *pranayama*.

Practice of Prathyahara

❖ What is *prathyahara*? *Prathyahara* is that abstention by which the senses do not come into contact with their objects and follow, as it were, the nature of the (controlled) mind.

"When the mind is withdrawn from the sense objects the sense organs also withdraw themselves from their objects and they are said to imitate the mind. This is known as *prathyahara*."

❖ The entire secret of *prathyahara* is will-power, which every normal person is capable of developing; but in most people it is in an undeveloped state. When confirmed in *prathyahara* one attains mastery over one's senses, thoughts and emotions.

Practice of *prathyahara* helps develop will-power.

—**The Mind and its Control**

Swami Budhananda

Five Phases of Mental Development

❖ Development of the power of concentration, the capacity for attention.

❖ Development of the capacities of expansion, widening, complexity and richness.

❖ Organisation of one's ideas around a central idea, a higher ideal or a supremely luminous idea that will serve as a guide in life.

❖ Thought-control, rejection of undesirable thoughts, the ability to think only what one wants and when one wants.

❖ Development of mental silence, perfect calm and a more and more total receptivity to inspirations coming from the higher regions of the being.

— *The Mother*

Importance of Meditation

❖ Meditations on God is the most effective way of controlling the mind. Meditation and control of the mind go hand in hand. The highest objective for which one controls the mind is meditation on God or *Atman* as the case may be. However, meditation also helps control of the mind.

❖ The mind must be riveted on something which is not only pure in itself but can also purify our mind through its power. Meditation of God, is advised, because one becomes imbued with the quality of the object on which one meditates.

- ❖ In meditation, whenever the mind strays away one should indefatitably bring it back and place it on the object of meditation.

Guided Meditation

❖ Let us for a few minutes sit quietly, relax our body and mind. Let us now sit in a straight posture: and send a current of thoughts in all directions— East, West, North and South — and mentally repeat:

Let all beings be happy; let all beings be peaceful; let all beings be blissful."

❖ Let us offer our salutation to the Supreme, all-pervading, all-blissful Divine Spirit who dwells in the hearts of us all. Out of Him, the all-pervading, all-blessing Divine Spirit, we all have come into being; in Him we live, to Him we return. Let us offer our salutation to Him. May He guide our understanding.

❖ Let us now do a little *Pranayama* by way of breathing in and breathing out. While inhaling, let us think that we are drawing within ourselves purity, compassion, strength, courage and other godly virtues. While exhaling, let us think that we are ejecting, from within, all imperfections, such as evil thoughts, impurity, narrowness, envy and sinful tendencies.

❖ Let us now take up the position of the witness or spectator and draw our mind from all directions. Let us detach ourselves from everything that is non-Atman. Let us close our eyes and fix our consciousness in the sanctuary of our heart and think that our chosen ideal in a shining form is residing there. Let us feel the Divine contact in our heart of hearts. May the Divine presence soothe our nerves, calm our mind, quiet our hearts. May the blessings of the Divine Spirit shine in the hearts of all mankind to usher in a new dawn so that men may forget hatred and misunderstanding, and strive towards spiritual awakening and cordial understanding. May the Divine Spirit bless us to build a solid structure of the human family, on the firm basis of mutual trust, faith and loving harmony.

❖ In the end, let us pray to the Almighty to help us to spread His fragrance everywhere we go. Let Him flood our soul with His spirit and love. Let Him penetrate and possess our whole being so utterly that all our life may only be a radiance of Him. Let Him shine through us in such a manner that every soul we come in contact with may feel His presence in our soul. Let people look up and see us no longer, but only the Almighty.

❖ May the all-pervading, all-blissful spirit, the soul of our souls protect us, may He guide us all, may He, out of His infinite Mercy, destroy all our sins, faults, wants and miseries, root and branch, so that we may awaken the infinite power which is lying dormant within us, so that we may realise our true nature — the eternal, ever-pure, ever free, ever-luminous self.

Om! Peace be within and without, everywhere!

Peace be to all beings; Peace be on earth and all the spheres of the Heavens!

Om Shanti, Shanti, Shanti Om!

— *Swami Gokulananda*